D0823667

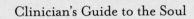

Clinician's Guide to the Soul

Veneta Masson

Clinician's Guide
to the
Soul

I imagined poetry might,
if given the chance,
even heal medicine itself.

— Rafael Campo, *The Healing Art*

Copyright © 2008 by Veneta Masson
First Edition
ISBN 978-0-9673688-2-5

Library of Congress Control Number
2007905266

Printed in the United States of America
by HBP, Inc., Hagerstown MD

All rights reserved.

Please address inquiries to:
Sage Femme Press
PO Box 32124
Washington, DC 20007

www.sagefemmepress.com

Art by Rachel Dickerson

Design by Lisa Carey Design, LLC
www.lisacareydesign.com

Dear Reader,

Though I want to think I know something about you, and you about me, let's assume we don't.

I was a caregiver before I was a poet. For thirty-five years, I worked as a registered nurse in communities, homes and hospitals both in the United States and abroad. It was my job with an international health organization that landed me in Washington, D.C. And it was a chance to do primary care in one of Washington's inner-city neighborhoods that drew me away from what I had thought would be a career in international health.

As a family nurse practitioner, crammed into the provider office of our small clinic with Jim Hall, MD and Teresa Acquaviva, RN, FNP for most of two decades, I gained a deeper understanding and appreciation of the physician's role as well as the nurse's. I thought a lot about what healing is, how we as healers practice our art, how we understand and apply science, and how our roles are shaped by language, culture, politics, economics and the people who entrust themselves to our care. I've also experienced my share of family illness and death. Through the years, I've addressed these themes in poems and essays.

In my practice, I relied on countless "clinician's guides," concise, up-to-the-minute print or online references on specific topics like antibiotics, common skin conditions or pediatric lab values. But a guide to the soul! What is the soul? And why, in this age of scientific exploration and achievement, do so many of us insist on its relevance to health and health care?

In his book, *Care of the Soul*, Thomas Moore writes, "Soul is not a thing, but a quality or a dimension of experiencing life and ourselves. It has to do with depth, value, relatedness, heart, and personal substance." Perhaps that's why I believe the title that came to me for this collection is apt.

It's my hope that nurses and physicians will find sustenance, healing and the occasional flash of recognition in these poems. But if they were letters, I'd also send them to patients, family caregivers, health workers of all kinds, readers of poetry and, most especially, you.

Faithfully,

Veneta Masson

Contents

The Poet's Job

*The poet can't change anything, but the poet can
demonstrate the power of the solitary conscience.*
—*Stanley Kunitz*

Even herded into plurals—
    Poets Against the War
    Poets for Human Rights—
poets don't make headlines or laws,
don't discover the next wonder drug or
renewable energy source.

    But they are equipped
    to do practical work.
    After science, art and religion
    have their messy say,
    poets pick through the clutter—
    questions, suppositions, certainties—

    then abscond with their stash to
    that vast recycling bin
    where, parsed into singulars,
    they ply their slow trade
    in words, images, mystery—
    tinkers of the imagination.

Their poems may end on the ash heap
though the divine combustion
has been known to light up a city
or, like a disposable penlight,
guide one or two souls down
   the dark path
     to their own door.

WANTING MEMORIES
RACHEL DICKERSON

Fortune

1. A journey must begin   Yes, let it begin
   with a single step   the sacramental breaking of cookie

2. Don't be afraid to   trust the tiny article of faith inside
   take that big step   find riches, fame, romance

3. If you can't decide   let fortune guide you
   up or down   to the edge of reason
   try moving across   that beguiling divide

4. Many a false step   full of portent
   is made by standing still   jump

Passages

Tragic! the day shift said that afternoon when I came on duty.
She's 35 and dying of uterine cancer.
Yes, he's still there, sitting beside her—

> he seems to want us to leave them alone.

Imagine how he must feel, after all

> a gynecologist
>
> watching his wife
>
> die on account of his impotence.

At least she's too far gone to feel the pain.

Tragic! I echoed, looked down at my feet

> stuffed my notes and my hands into pockets.

At 20, I was a novice still

> and ill at ease
>
> with the celebration
>
> of mysteries.

Reluctantly, I began my rounds, knowing that door

> at the end of the hall
>
> was one I had to open.

The moment came. I knocked lightly and entered.
First I saw her, or rather the barely perceptible

> rise and fall
> of the caul
> of luminous sheets.

Then I saw him, eyes fixed on the IV drip

> as if on an hour glass
> watching the last few
> grains of sand run through.

I want to talk with you, he said as I worked

> then followed me out when I left the room.

Where in God's name have you been? he exploded.
For hours no one has opened that door!

> And then in a small
> and stubbed out voice

How do you know if she's dead or alive?
There's nobody with her but me.

> *I'm sorry,* I said, and stood there.

He was 40, a physician, and powerless
                    to stop this traitor womb
                    from giving birth to death.
I wanted to say, but hadn't the words
                    What can I do?
                    You are the healer.
I didn't know then the things I know now about how it is
                    that nurses heal
                    and healers fail

                    and face the face of loss again and again.
Many times I've wanted to find him, touch him
                    as I couldn't do then
                    let his eyes sink into mine
                    hear him down to the roots of his words
                    practice now familiar rites of nurturance.
                    And yet, if he asked, I would have to confess
                    I am 40, a healer, and still don't know
                    a remedy for despair.

The Promise

If you could just lose weight
your blood pressure would go down
your diabetes would clear up
you could get off all those pills you take
your joints wouldn't ache
you could climb the stairs
run after the bus
carry the groceries
pick up the baby
the swelling in your legs would go down
you could reach all the way to your aching feet
you could breathe again

You could find clothes to fit
get out of those slippers and into real shoes
who knows but what your old man would come back
you'd get more respect from your children
a decent job
your son would kick drugs
your daughter wouldn't get pregnant again
you'd live to see your last one grown

Your neighbors wouldn't talk about you
the toilet would flush
the roof wouldn't leak
there'd be food enough at the end of the month
they wouldn't cut off your check
jack up the rent
you'd hit the number
go off for two weeks in Aruba

> Jesus would save the world from sin
> those who mourn would be comforted
> the poor would enter the Kingdom of God
> your hunger would be filled.

Admission

Her eyes would blur
so she couldn't see
to fill the syringes.
Often as not
she'd skip the dose
and damn the diabetes.

She'd get groggy
so she'd lose her balance
        and fall—
bound to break a hip one day
land in the hospital
die of complications.

                The most complicated things
                are simple
                in the beginning.

I offer a house call
to check her sugar
and fill the syringes
a week at a time.

I offer to enter
once every week
an uncharted world
not my own.

Enter, do for, exit
Simple!
Enter, look around, listen
do for, exit

Enter, wonder
Enter, ask

Enter deeper
Enter

Rx

Politicians... were quick to rise to the defense of a particularly vulnerable population. As a group, dual-eligibles [Medicare-Medicaid] have incomes below the poverty rate... and take an average of 15 medications a day.

— *Washington Post*

This is how it works:
as wealth trickles down
to the poor and old
it turns into pills.

So M and S, their slender portfolios
long since depleted, can still
compete for bragging rights.
I take twenty a day, says M.
Ha! counters S, *I take so many
they had to put in a port.*

G presides over the corporate enterprise,
his specialty, mergers and acquisitions.
With combined assets (his own and his wife's)
filling two cupboards, he allocates resources,
tracks inventory, restocks
from Wal-Mart and Canada.

K can still indulge herself.
I'll start with one of the pale pink ones,
she tells the striped tabby,
but I might decide I need two or three.
I'll wait a while and see how I feel.
Maybe the purple would do me more good.

Honor is served.
Wealth is transferred.
The old have their pills.
And their health?
That's another story.

The Screamer in Room 4

This toddler glares at me
from her mother's lap.
Her eyes are sharp as tacks
black as coals.
She greets me with a scream
will not let me touch her
or cajole a momentary lull
in the hostilities.
Mother does not intervene
makes no apologetic coos
no irritated reprimand
no sound at all.

Are we playing house?

Let's see, mommy is high
and daddy went bye-bye
before you were born
and mommy's new friend
has a violent streak
brother is hyper

CALMING THE BEAST WITHIN
RACHEL DICKERSON

big sister won't speak
grandma is angry
but what can she do?
So who does that make you
little screamer?
Who does that make you?

The Secret Life of Nurses

You won't read about it in the tabloids
or inside the gaudy jacket of a Harlequin.
Dear Abby knows nothing about it.
Priests and lovers may think they do
and you
as you glimpse the tips of their shoes
                    stalled outside a door—
you may think you do,
but you don't.

Nurses keep a safe house hidden
in the spaciousness of imagination—
            a dark kiva dug into
                    the sun-bleached cliff
            a gracious ark
                    gliding high on still waters
            a lavender planet idling among far stars.

They keep a safe house
and a fleet of neurons poised for flight.

Incidental Finding

suspicious for malignancy

Say I've lost a button,
one of a kind,
from a garment I must wear.
I search the closet, the dusty floor,
shine a flashlight under the bed.
No button there, but something
scuttling away from the light—
insect, arachnid, artifact?

> What does it want?
> Will it bite, or merely haunt?

That night I lie uneasy,
my clean white sheets no longer safe.
I dream I'm pursued by carnivorous
buttons, arise hollow-eyed
rewash the sheets
buy a new mattress, pillow and spread,
exterminate, consider
prying out floorboards.

> You pay a steep price for safety.
> It's one of the more expensive illusions.

Witness

Sunday
after church
under a sleeve of summer sky
we walk up the alley
called Wiltberger Street
look down
at the blood-stained cement.

He was fourteen
on just another
hip hop high top
Saturday
in the hood when
somebody put his lights out—
semiautomatic.

The people who live
on the alley
behind brick façades
won't talk
but lock up their kids
for the weekend.
They could be next.

I want to kneel
in this stagnant pool
of spent rage,
smear the blood all over
my face, my clothes
and wander like Cain
through the city and say

Look at me and see
what I have seen.

But I don't.
I stay where I am,
nursing wounds
that never heal for want
of the capacity to feel—
like ulcers on a sole
bereft of sensation.

What balm is there
in this violent Gilead
to make the wounded whole?
I know no cure
and all I have is breath
a voice
and memory—

memory
a voice.

Guilt

The ER phones with
a sick little girl
under your care for a year
and now
critical
with surgery
standing by.

>*What can I do?*
>*My daughter is dying!*
>the mother had said
>two months ago
>and again and again,
>but tests showed
>nothing.

Just look at her!
the mother said.
I did, and saw
the light
in those mischievous eyes
dimming out, drowned
in maternal anxiety.

Questions, regrets
hang in the air—
and guilt,
like a vise with jaws
that crush compassion,
frets at objectivity,
diminishes all it touches.

They've got no case,
I've done no harm,
I think as I voice
concern,
and every growing
part of me chars down
to a hard dark cinder.

Lower Midline Surgical Scar

I see so many
so many scarred women
who cannot tell me
why they were cut
what was taken or
how it changed them.

They say
    There was a tumor...
    I bled...
    The pain...
    I was pregnant...
    I'm not really sure...

I touch these scars
one by one
day after day,
describe them all
in the same four words
for the record.

Is there more to say
or feel
about a minor breach
of integrity
in a complex body
of evidence?

Well healed, I might write—
the clinician's
seal of approval.
But how do I know
what lies below
the surface—

still palpable relief,
benign regret,
anxiety,
or a hot and throbbing memory
that rankles wordlessly
within?

Gold Standard

Ensure that the drug information you rely on is as good as gold by adopting Alchemy, the superior clinical decision support engine from Gold Standard.
—*www.alchemyrx.com*

Strange alchemy indeed—
money to medicine
banking to science—
the gold standard transmuted.
Its appeal is irresistible.
What athlete or patient sets his sights
on the silver or bronze?
And as for clinicians,
we have to stake our claim
somewhere. Precious few will reveal
the only thing they know for sure—
that there is no Fort Knox,
only an Oz where wizards
come and go.

When I think of all the pyrite
I've proffered through the years—
the abandoned theories,
discredited pills and procedures,
unsubstantiated advice—
all of it gold standard,
I make my confession
and offer this prayer
to the God of Unknowing,
Lord, make me your placebo,
a humble purveyor
of sensible care,
a healer who never fails,
at least, to give a damn.

Rescue

"Everyone is shining their flashlights, so as you're flying over, it's kind of like you see a sky full of sparkling stars. So which star do you pick?"

—Helicopter pilot, after Hurricane Katrina

It's no more random than anything else in life.
Think of all those lights shining in the dark—
the children of famine holding up their empty bowls,
the battle wounded waiting for a medic,
the homeless milling outside the overcrowded shelter,
the hapless victims held at gunpoint,
the sick lying on their pallets at Bethesda,
the dying trapped by fire, flood, earthquake, avalanche,
the living.

Rescue, if it comes, is only temporary.
The pilots, medics, aid workers, police—
so few, so fallible.
But high above them the Creator of Light
patrols the dark, counting the stars.
None are missed, all accounted for.

Understanding the Plot

Impossible that I should forget
the plot, but here I am, lost
       among the stone pages
       of this sprawling book of lives.
       I have no desire to browse.
       Only one story interests me.

       I find the marker at last.
       Two strangers with vases
       stand there reading,
       nod their heads slowly, plod on.
               What is it they know
               that I have yet to learn?

       Though I can't see their faces,
       the vases they carry
       speak volumes. Empty,
       done for now with their holding,
       ready once again to receive,
       they tell their silent parable.

Dwell Time

*The average time from onset of a polyp to onset
of carcinoma, termed the "dwell time"....*
                    —American Family Physician

There in a lumen devoid of light
   downstream from the churning river of chyme and industry
      the tiny pedunculate dwells on its stalk

couched in paradox.
   Granted potential, it serves no purpose—
      artist without a medium, builder without a blueprint.

Dreaming in the velvet darkness called innocence,
   the neophyte knows nothing of beauty or biology,
      the oyster's pearl or the ancient spruce's extravagant burl.

Its impulse is pure, the outcome uncertain.
   What lies between genesis and revelation
      is called the dwell time.

AMONG THE TREES
RACHEL DICKERSON

The Doctor's Laptop

The day came when not even paper
passed between us. A laptop appeared
on the vast expanse of desktop
that had always stood
between my doctor and me.
It gulped down my story—
an indigestible slurry
of symptoms, dates and question marks—
with impatient clicks
and short, skeptical pauses.

It preceded us into the exam room
where it sat with its back to my nakedness
in a pointed show of disinterest,
then led us again to the room with the desk.
There, in silence,
it assigned diagnoses
researched best practices
sent referrals
prescriptions
instructions
insurance forms

and the date of my next appointment
to linked computers and printers
in distant locations.

I envy the laptop its capacity, certainty
and complete absence of need.
I envy it my doctor's thoughtful touch,
attentive gaze,
and the deference it gets—
though it hasn't the wit
to fancy itself a healer,
or wise.

If You Didn't Chart It

If you didn't chart it,
you didn't do it.
Straightforward advice
to the risk averse,
duly noted.
So I write things like this:

> Preventive screening scheduled
> Return if symptoms persist
> Referred for specialty consult
> Counseled regarding side effects
> Risks of procedure explained
> Informed consent obtained.

But that time you came in
with symptoms that scared you
half out of your skin and I listened hard
but hadn't a clue so stayed up
all night combing through journals
calling up colleagues,

finally confided what I'd do
if I were you, that I'd see you through
whatever it took, gave you my number,
came in after hours
and you made it, thank god?
That never happened.

Pathology Report

The specimens	Parts of me
are received	cut from their moorings
in two containers	floating placidly
specimen No. 1	lifted out
labeled	by dispassionate hands
ovary	measured, weighed
the external surface	splayed on a countertop
distorted	so much
by a large	once secret
cystic structure	now exposed
filled with	old
dark	imperfections
reddish-brown	festering
material	like a failed heart
specimen No. 2	large, scarred
labeled	utterly useless
uterus	no matter that
opening reveals	a creation of sorts
a mass	suggestive of life
with fleshy-pink	formed
whorled surface	inside
the cavity	which
is compressed	at last
by the mass	cut to the quick
representative sections	proved counterfeit
are submitted	stillborn

Refuge

The eternal God is thy refuge,
and underneath are the everlasting arms....
*   —Deuteronomy 33:27*

From the stagnant pool of futility
the pitiless ocean of grief
the unshepherded valley of lost sheep
the desert of reluctant unbelief—
from these lonesome places
I call to you, my waning god.

I don't ask to hear your voice,
                    see your face,
                    know your mind.

I don't ask.

I want only the rough embrace
of the everlasting arms
and in this primitive grace
to find refuge.

Where There's One

there's more than one—
you can bet your life

Take the lone cockroach
who flits into view
when you flip on the kitchen light
one starved for sleep night
your heart sinks
doesn't it

And when you find
that first gray hair
magnified in the bathroom mirror
one incandescent morning
you root it out in despair
don't you

Termites
hives
infidelities
lies
they don't come in ones

So when the surgeon concedes
there's reason to hope—
only one positive node—
you know the divide
between none and one
is infinite
whereas with one—
where there's one
you simply can't believe
only

What it comes down to
is lack of faith.
Why not an errant cockroach?
Why not a single gray hair?

You have a conversion experience.

Treatment Plan

How old is your youngest?
the doctor asked.

Seven
        she said.

So young
        he said.

She bowed her head
   said
   nothing.

He put down his pen
   raised his head
   waited.

Did you know that

healing begins
   in the pupil
   of the eye?

"i think my life is changing,"

she said softly.

She closed her eyes and fell asleep.

Conga! at the Rio

for Rebecca

She's sick but determined
to celebrate my coming
for the second round of chemo.

She stuffs her bra with shoulder pads
dons a long gown and a honey blonde wig
takes her anti-nausea pill.

You're crazy, I say
eyeing her with angst and admiration
but it's clear she won't be swayed,

so we set off for the Strip
and the show she's chosen,
"Conga! at the Rio."

We're asked to dance. I decline.
Dare I take pleasure at such a time?
I shake my head no—

even as she's nodding hers yes.
She gathers herself and goes,
dances the finale center stage.

Every life has a theme
and this is mine: I am the nurse,
the soul of compassion

                    with much still to learn about
                    freeing my passion and kissing
                    joy as it flies.

We head for home in a haze of regret,
she, for the dance, over too soon,
me, for missing another chance.

Cure

In Latin it means care,
conjures priests and temples
the laying on of hands
sacred pilgrimage
sacrifice
the sickbed
invalid and
solemn attendants.

How far we have come.
Today's English
has neatly expunged
these purely human elements.
Cure is impersonal, consequential
unequivocal, sometimes violent—
the annihilation
of the thing that ails.

This nurse
approaching the patient
has discarded temple garb
for practical scrubs.
His gloved hands
unsheathe the magic bullet,
shoot it through the central line
where it locks onto the target cells.

For the not-yet-cured,
there is still sacred pilgrimage—
that dogged slog
to the high tech shrine,
the health food store,
the finish line of the annual race
where, etched on each undaunted face,
is a gritty tale of survival.

Cancer Clinic

USA
The glare of tile and fluorescence
illuminates this windowless bay
where from each deep recliner
there is nowhere to look but up
at wall-mounted TVs.
Infusions infuse
a centrifuge spins
sheathed voices confide
brief messages
and all along the long hall
    doors open
    doors close.

Germany
Gemütlichkeit
and brisk good cheer
breach a broad expanse
of desk and theory.
The theories spin out
in long tangled skeins
riddled with promise and caution.
You unravel the skeins
then thread your way

to the quaint, timbered apothecary.
    Prepare yourself
    for the bitter taste
    of hope.

            Mexico
            An old man sings
            and plays his guitar
            while diners
                pacientes, compañeros, médicos
            forage among the bright gleaming greens
            in search of purification.
            At long tables they partake of their lean feast
            while the old man sings.

            The old man who sings
            wears a lab coat.
            The old man who sings
            is the *jefe.*
            The old man is strong
            and his song is sweet.
                Take, eat, *mis pacientes,*
                then drift to your rooms
                and dream of serene old age.

Negative Conditioning

At first it was just the needles she hated
she had bad veins
and good instincts.

Then she began to hate her doctor
his face, set like an alarm clock
his merciless attention to time.

In time, the sight of the fish tank in the waiting room
made her sick
that queasy medium
those darting appraisals—piscine and human—
from the other side of the glass

and the elevator
sealing her off, in
before she had pushed the button
before she was ready

and the short walk from the parking lot
in spite of the glare
a fog of premonition

and the drive from home
no longer behind the wheel
no longer in control

> even leaving the house
> saying goodbye
> shutting the door behind her
> each time
> a rehearsal.

OFFERING, RACHEL DICKERSON

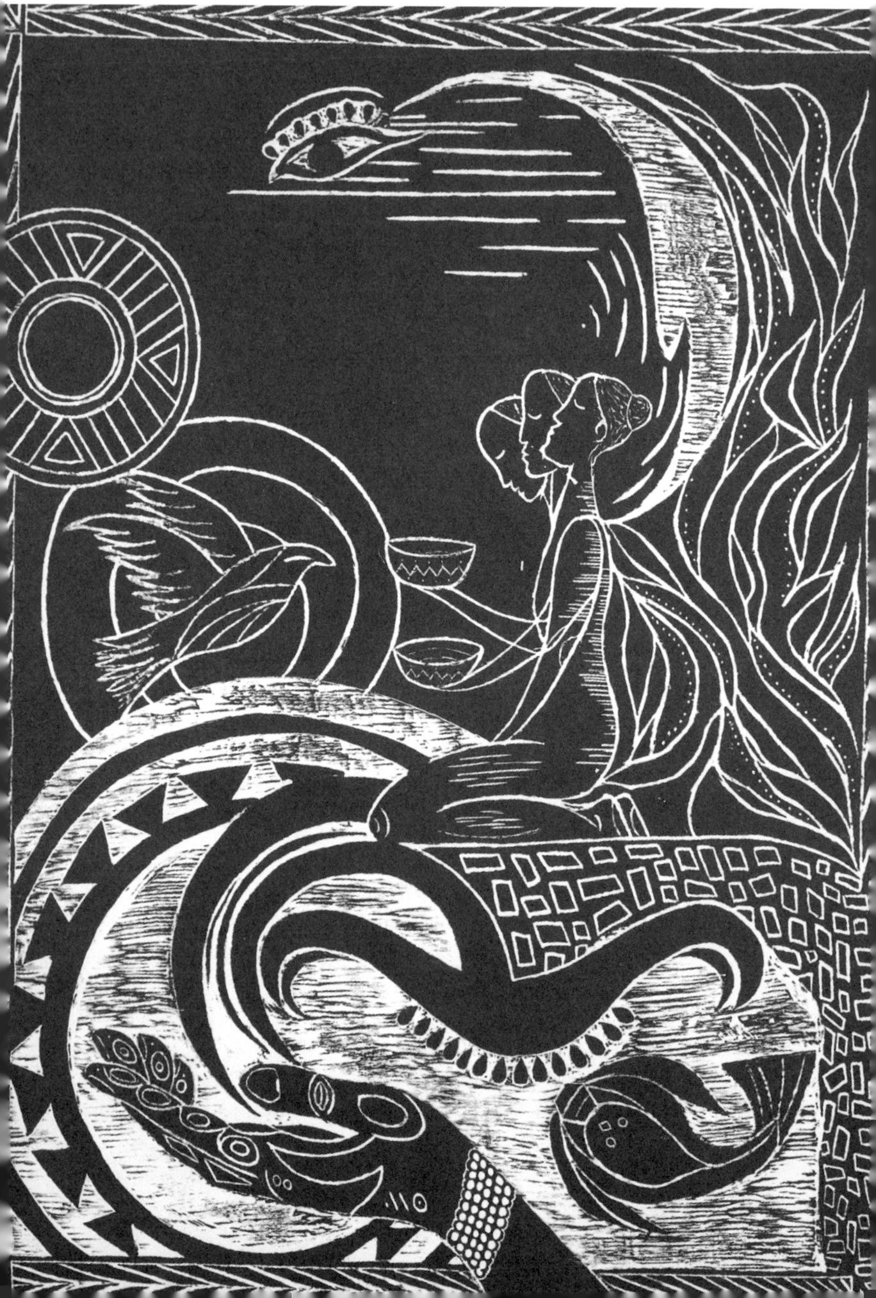

The Next Island

...that untraveled world whose margin fades
forever and forever when I move.
                    —Alfred, Lord Tennyson

After the third round of chemo
she flew to Hawaii and
after the fourth, to Barbados.
She's not the first to push
beyond the tottering arc of fate
toward the gleaming, untraveled world.

Back in her desert, she dreams
about the next island.
When, where, how and how much
doesn't matter as much
as the fact that it's out there, singing
through the sun like Bali H'ai.

Why resign yourself
to a short life in time
when there must be
an eternity of islands?

Metastasis

from Late Latin, transition, from Greek, meta–
(involving change) + histanai (cause to stand)

The trip to Paradise
was planned well before
the recurrence
manifested itself
cunningly
like sleight of hand—
now here, now there—
among the once vital
organs.

> After a brief flurry of indecision—
> more-chemo-what-the-hell
> or a peek at Paradise—
> she chose the latter
> as having perhaps the better claim
> because it was classy
> and wouldn't she fare
> a lot better on an island in the sun
> than head down in a toilet bowl
> flushed
> with toxins?

Knowing how way leads on to way
she went
and, sure enough,
basking there
in Paradise,
she sighed and said
If only I never had to go back...

I tell you this: metastasis
was a magical word
before cancer
got hold of it.
It could transform you.
Still can.

Collateral Damage

He was lucky alright.
They caught it early
and he was ready to fight.
The treatment was brutal.
Left him with a melted gut, bad lungs
and feet like cement blocks.
Never be the same, he says,
wonders if it was worth it.
No sex life now. You can imagine.
But he's alive a year later and
that tells you something.

Carpe diem—
isn't that how they say it in Latin?
Or do I mean *caveat emptor?*

The Science of Comforting

for Jan Morse

It's not a crowded field.
After all, there's no Nobel
for achievement in caregiving,
no headlines to grab. Want
grants, tenure, a plush lab?
Then work on the genome,
stem cells, a cure for death.

But suppose some sick bloke,
suffering despite his fortune,
decided to endow
a Consolation Prize.
Tell me, which nurse
would you nominate?

Home From the Doctor's

for Ron

Home from the doctor's
the day she learned it had gone to her brain

           she sat at the white baby grand
           and played

the children's lessons spangled with stars,
hymns, easy pieces she knew by heart—

           her healing art.
           Mindlessly, she fingered the keys,

those narrow skiffs she knew could bear
the weight of her uncertainty

and carry her into that buoyant sea where
music beguiles mortality.

Clinician

from the Greek klinē, bed

Golf, tennis
even jazz has them now—
the cat who comes to hear you play,
hone your chops and
find your truth.

But it started with us,
nurses, physicians
hunched over the sickbed,
bringing to bear our senses,
skill, intelligence—

purely human, fallible.
No help from silicon chips,
telemetry, robotics.
I can still catch a glimpse
in the rear view mirror.

Those were the days
when your instrument was you,
when every patient's truth
was his own.

Poem of the Week

A friend's sage advice:
Just do what you can do
on a given day.
So on days I can't pray
or pick up the phone
I send a poem.
Poem of the Weak,
I once accidentally called it.

I've sent Carver, Frost
Sarton, Levertov
Pastan, Olds and others—
my emissaries
my cloud of witnesses.

Let these poets earn their keep.
Let them speak for me.
Let them enter the house
haunted by illness.
Let them open the doors
shut against fear.

UNTITLED
RACHEL DICKERSON

For in trouble
the poem is strong medicine
like the wind that blows
where it wills,
like the serpent of brass
set upon a pole
in the wilderness.

Leaving the Mainstream

We are leaving the mainstream.
We are swimming as fast as we can
away from the pain
the poison
the blustery promises
empty as air.

We swim hard against the tide
but it is strong
and sweeps us along
the moment we lose momentum.

Those we leave behind
with gaping mouths
and blinking eyes
recede into the distance,
stranded on the shoals
of failed persuasion

but we swim on, propelled
by instinct and fear toward
the ocean of possibility,
vast, wild, supremely indifferent.
It is there, out of our depth,
sinking fast, that we first see light—

bright quick flicks
in a rainbow of colors
cutting a wide ragged
swath in the sea.
Ah! A new school!
We join it.

Safe for now and full of hope
we scarcely attend
to those arrogant sharks
ringing the perimeter.

They bide their time
waiting for signs of trouble—
brief founderings,
the unraveling of resolve.

Matinée

Still sisters, we get into the car.
We've just seen a movie.
In it, the heroine dies in her prime.
We knew she would.

Maybe that's why we went.
It's easier to talk about the heroine
who dies than about the sister
who will.

We sit in the darkening
parking garage waiting for words.
I flick a speck from an eyelash.
She turns to pick at a sleeve.

Usually we work from a script.
Her part is full of silences,
mine, of incomplete sentences.
But this scene is pure improv.

I'm afraid, she ventures.
Me too, I confess.
Though not dying, I'm her witness
and must testify.

Neither of us is a heroine
though one will die in her prime.
We didn't know she would.
This is a different matinée.

Hilda and Snow White

These are not our real names.
They are secret names
        play names
        names from an intimate
        afternoon game.

I am Hilda, the faithful nurse.
Snow White is nine,
the wise and beautiful daughter.
The good mother is very ill
        in a far room
        on a dark wing
        of the castle.
She may die.

Snow White knows this.
She knows this and the rest of the story.
There will be a wicked stepmother
        a poisoned apple
        a death-like trance
        a grieving, ineffectual father
        a prince
No!
Yes, why not?

A prince.

She'd like to believe
this is all make-believe
a fairy tale
but failing that
        she'd like to believe
        in princes.

AMATERASU
RACHEL
DICKERSON

The Nurse's Job

"...with Mom so sick and everyone asking
where's her sister, the nurse..."

The nurse's job is to make it better
whatever it is
(even a child knows this)
to smooth the forest of furrowed brows
to explain pathologies and pain
to say it will be all right
when it will
and when it won't
to relieve, to be there, to stay.

I have failed at my job.
Even a child knows this.
I offer sporadic intensive care
long-distance counsel
and two thousand miles of excuses.
My absence must smack of
malpractice.

And yet, in the end
there is sanctuary at St. Rose.
As two nurses wedge
between me and her bed
I know I can't distance myself again.
I cling to the rails
confess that I, too, am a nurse.

> *You're not a nurse here,*
> *you're her sister*
> one says, swaddling me
> tight in her arms.
> I believe she has loved a sister.
> I believe that she has known shame.

She does not say
it will be all right
but in her presence
I give in to grief
I begin to let go.
This nurse is doing her job.

La Muerte

*If Muerte comes and sits down beside you,
you are lucky, because Death has chosen to teach
you something.*

—Clarissa Pinkola Estes

Old Mother Death sits
down beside me.
Neither cruel nor kind
she does not take, she receives.
We are, all of us, her wards.
Contrary to what you may think
she is in no hurry.
Only humans fret about time.
She squats close to the earth
knees spread wide in a generous lap
and there, mossy shawl drawn
close about her, she waits, shuffling
the letters of her strange alphabet.
I see her fingerpads smudged with ink.
I edge closer.
I am ready to learn.

Upheaval

Months have passed
since death struck
shattering everything fragile
collapsing carefully crafted structures.

Now, like tectonic plates
after an earthquake,
relationships shift and resettle
in a series of startling aftershocks.

Smooth surfaces crack.
Rifts form, and deep depressions.
Their familiar terrain disrupted,
all learn to tread carefully.

Homes are rebuilt or relocated.
There are new couplings,
the next generation forms.
The survivors survive

but, on the seismograph
of each human heart,
a register remains of every time
it stopped to add a name.

IN HER GLORY
RACHEL DICKERSON

Doubtless

for Doris

This dense nebula
of tiny blackpoll warblers

sensing the shortness of the light,
ready to lift into flight—

surely there are skeptics among them—

the one who flies out of formation
there at the ragged edge

the one who never leads
nor seems to follow

the one who tails behind
but rises nonetheless

no heavier than a soul

and at journey's end
arrives, doubtless, with the rest.

Placebo

One time it was
a black paste from India
putrid as sulphur fumes.
She'd dose herself
from the small unmarked jar
with the tip of a toothpick
and gag it down
with hunks of bread.
It was expensive
and came from dear friends
who knew of cures
or had heard
or read...

For a time she thought
she felt better.
Surely anything so vile
must be redemptive.
Besides, this could be
her last tribute to friendship—

>   *Despite my unease*
>   *I shall please,*
>   *I shall please.*

Buying Time

for Frank

My friend is sick.
The doctors can't
promise a cure
but think they can buy
more time.
Yes, more time!

We say *Time heals all,*
just give it time —
and yet now
is far more
than we know
what to do with.

Each life makes its arc
then glides out of time
slipping all ties. Pain dies.
Desire dies. Gone,
the humming dread
of what waits beyond breath.

Between time and release
the space is vast, serene.
Linger there,
dear friend,
till you shed
your need.

Prevention

They that be whole need not a physician,
but they that are sick.
                    —Matthew 9:12

I'm sitting in the dentist's chair.
I don't have a toothache.
I'm not in for repairs.
My mouth is full of the
implements of prevention.

Holding onto these teeth
and my few purchased immunities
is all I hope for by way of
preventive intervention.
The rest is the nerve-wracking search for IT
which, if found in time, with luck,
will be treatable.

Jesus, himself a healer
of bodies and souls,
did not worry himself with the well.
A prophet, he knew that all flesh is grass,
that nothing human will last and yet

even Jesus wanted to live.
If he preached today, would he
advocate colonoscopy,
cholesterol checks? We only know
that he died in his prime,
the price of his search
for a different IT.

Reference Range

Your tests show
the numbers 73, 90, 119 and 2.5,
the letter A,
the color yellow,
a straight line interrupted by a repeating pattern
of steeples and languid waves,
a gray asymmetrical oval
filled with fine white tracery,
35 seconds,
100 millimeters,
II.

I'm not sure what to make of these.
With the possible exception of II.,
which like all Roman numerals
is subject to misinterpretation,
I see no cause for alarm.
I admit to a preference for low numbers,
the apothecary system over the metric
(my age, perhaps, and distrust of pure logic)
and the letter W,
though most of my colleagues favor
M.

I think you can be happy with yellow
and, based on my experience,
the fact that the straight line is punctuated.
Seconds, millimeters—I marvel at their finitude,
but this oval, so intricate, so light,
might well contain a universe.
Is it normal, you ask.
Normal's a shell game you seldom win.
Take my advice. Enjoy good health
not as your due but the blessing it is
like Spring, laughter,
death.

Winter Count

Among several tribes on the northern plains, the passage of time from one summer to the next was marked by noting a single memorable event. The sequence of such memories…was called a winter count.
—*Barry Lopez*

WINTER
RACHEL DICKERSON

1958   Future Nurses Club. Junior High. We are photographed
        outside the clinic cottage wearing white caps.
        Becoming a nurse has somehow occurred to me.

1959   YMCA Medical Seminar. We tour the coroner's office
        in Los Angeles. I see naked bodies in long rows,
        think of the frogs we dissected in biology lab.

1960   Junior Volunteer. I push the water cart. A patient's call
        light blips on. I am terrified of what may be asked of me.
        Patient asks for water.

1961   In my senior yearbook, Mr. Olson writes "Doctor!
        I'll expect to hear of your accomplishments." Becoming
        a doctor has never occurred to me.

1962   The two comatose ladies in 360. I am the nursing
        student assigned to them each clinical day. I learn to
        talk to them but do not wonder about their lives.

1963   I am immobilizing a postop cataract patient with
        sandbags. Someone whispers that the President has been
        shot. I retreat to the linen closet.

1964   Dr. P yells at me in the hallway. His wife is dying.
She is our patient. I am the RN in charge. I do not
know how to respond.

1965   ER. Summer of the Watts riots. We attempt to
resuscitate an old woman whose skull was crushed in
a car crash. The doctor won't give up. Why?

1966   Back in school. I buy a paperback poetry collection
to read on the bus while commuting to class, discover
a poem called "Strokes." A door opens.

1967   Visiting Nurse. Walter is paraplegic, lewd, incorrigible.
Lives alone above a bar. Roaches flit across his calendar
girl's face, my shoes. I bathe him, fend him off.

1968   My stroke patient Mrs. J says if there's something in
life you want to do, do it now. She says she and her
husband waited too long. I go to Europe.

1969   Summer job. I am sent to cover ICU over dinner break.
First time in ICU. Feed patient dinner. We talk.
I like him. He dies. I am compelled to write about this.

1970   Grad school. We read Kafka's "Metamorphosis"
        in a nursing theory course. I find it bracing, baffling.
        What would it mean to wake up as a cockroach?

1971   My story about the death in ICU wins me a trip to the
        Bread Loaf Writers' Conference in Vermont where I
        learn that it is a bad story.

1972   Applied to work in international health. Wanted to
        go to Africa. Sent to Laredo, Texas. Still, it is *La Frontera.*

1973   Brazil, hospital ship. Brazilian nurses work as counterparts
        to Americans and bunk deep in the bowels of the ship.
        I have a private cabin and porthole.

1974   Brazil, the new hospital. We have no water. Doctors
        protest poor facilities by refusing to see patients,
        sit in their cars outside in parking lot.

1975   I meet Frank over cafezinho at the Brazilian-American
        Cultural Institute in Washington, D.C. We live in
        the same neighborhood, study Portuguese, marry.

1976   Guatemalan Highlands, after the earthquake. Cold in
        June. I am jolted out of bed in the middle of the night.
        Nurses are needed here but, above all, endurance.

1977   Morocco. Government officials want state of the art
        ICUs. One tells me he admires the American nurse.
        She is like the captain of a ship.

1978   Washington, D.C. Community Medical Care opens
        its doors. I am co-founder with Jim. We offer primary
        care and home care. It is a poor neighborhood.

1979   Christopher and Emma come for prenatal care. They
        have no insurance. Emma speaks no English. When Maria
        Carmen is born, I am asked to be godmother.

1980   I compare my work as nurse with Jim's as physician.
        He wears a lab coat. I do not. He narrows his focus.
        I cannot. I write these observations in a journal.

1981   My book on international nursing is published. It is bright
        orange with no cover art. I am pleased with the book
        but not its cover. A chapter of my life closes.

1982   Lease expires. We move in January. Pipes freeze in new clinic. Jim and I have falling out. He drives me home, wonders how we can continue to work together.

1983   Jim and I teach a course called "Healing the Whole Person." One session is on healing relationships. There are two on forgiveness.

1984   Lady Jane sits naked in her crowded apartment after the stroke. Tells me not to worry about money, a dollar a day is what she'll pay for home care.

1985   Maggie's old mutt traps me on the stairway as I try to leave her house. I have fed it, fed her. I am fed up. With strokes of my pen, I turn my anger into a poem.

1986   Margaret nods off on toilet seat in the clinic's only bathroom. All morning, patients and staff exercise continence. Margaret is a very mean drunk.

1987   I tell LM his HIV test has come back positive. He is our first positive. He is shaken. I learn to deliver bad news.

1988   I write columns for a nursing journal about life in the
clinic and health care in the United States. I write about
money, AIDS, doctors' work, nurses' work.

1989   I study medicine and pharmacology at the University.
It is both more and less complicated than the care of
real patients. I am certified as a nurse practitioner.

1990   I have surgery. My uterus is detached. I detach. Enjoy
sweet slow days on the front porch. My patient,
Ms. Mary, stumps up the front steps bearing cakes.

1991   I sit at the feet of Our Lady, Queen of Ireland, in the
Shrine. Baby Jesus is on her lap. My Salvadoran patients
grieve for the children they have left behind.

1992   Outward Bound. Rock-climbing above the Rio Grande.
I can't climb back up the way I came down. I learn to
look for another place on the rock.

1993   I try working evenings in Urgent Care at the HMO.
Dr. O greets me cheerfully, says she works well with
"midlevels." No footholds on this part of the rock.

1994   I wait with Rebecca in the pre-op hold area. R is
my sister. She has breast cancer. The room is cold.
Needle caps and spent bandages litter the floor.

1995   Lease expires. The clinic renews. I do not. Jim gives me
the pinecone he brought back from the retreat we led
at Big Bear Lake in California.

1996   Women's clinic. After examining L, I slide my notebook
out of the desk drawer, write "...the hush that falls
as my fingers hesitate over the left breast..."

1997   Jack and I drive Rebecca home after last ditch treatment
in Mexico. She is comatose. We get stuck at the border.
Buy *piñatas* for the children.

1998   I leave the women's clinic for study tour of traditional
healing in Navajo country. I do not return to it.
I will use my hands to write and to bless.

Rachel Dickerson and Her Art

I've known Rachel Dickerson since she was a child. We've been members of the same church community for more than twenty-five years. But I never guessed that she would blossom into an artist whose work would move me profoundly.

Two of the prints in this book hang in my home. "Wanting Memories" greets me when I open my front door and "Winter," which hangs in my bedroom, is the first thing I see when I open my eyes each morning. Both are, for me, healing.

Some people who see her art assume that Rachel is African American. She is not, but she grew up in the heart of Washington, D.C. and spent five formative months in Ghana. The title of "Wanting Memories," for example, comes from a song by Ysaye Maria Barnwell, composer and member of the iconic, Washington D.C.-based, African American female a cappella ensemble, "Sweet Honey in the Rock." The first line is, "I am sitting here wanting memories to teach me about the beauty of the world through my own eyes." Both the song and the print have influenced my writing.

"Winter" was created the same year my husband died. Something about its spaciousness and the convergence (or is it divergence?) of the lines evoke a sense of horizon, a path, and promise. I find it both stark and comforting.

I am grateful to Rachel for her presence in my life, her art and her willingness to let me use her prints in this book. It's my hope that they may "speak" to you in the same way poems do.

— *Veneta Masson*

First Appearances

"Admission," "Guilt," "Lower Midline Surgical Scar," in *Rehab at the Florida Avenue Grill* (1999, Sage Femme Press); "The Promise," "The Screamer in Room 4," and "Passages" also appear in this collection

"Cancer Clinic," "Where There's One," in *The Lancet*

"Conga! at the Rio," in *Rattle*

"Cure," "Reference Range," "Rx," in *Pulse*

"Doubtless," "If You Didn't Chart It," "The Promise," "The Screamer in Room 4" © *Journal of the American Medical Association,* reprinted with permission

"Fortune," "The Nurse's Job," "The Secret Life of Nurses," "Upheaval," in *Nursing Education Perspectives* (formerly *Nursing & Health Care Perspectives*)

"Gold Standard," in *The Healing Muse*

"Hilda and Snow White," in *RN*

"Home From the Doctor's," "Negative Conditioning," "Placebo," in the *American Journal of Nursing*

"La Muerte," in the *Journal of Medical Humanities*

"Leaving the Mainstream," in *Unbearable Uncertainty* (2000, Pioneer Valley Breast Cancer Network)

"Metastasis," in the *International Journal of Human Caring*

"Passages," in *Nursing Spectrum*

"Pathology Report," © *Annals of Internal Medicine,* reprinted with permission

"Poem of the Week," in *The Cancer Poetry Project* (2001, Fairview Press)

"Rescue," in *Hurricane Blues: Poems about Katrina and Rita* (2006, Southeast Missouri State University Press)

"Witness," in *Faith at Work*